SOMERSET
Wit & Humour

DREW STANTON

BRADWELL
BOOKS

Published by Bradwell Books
9 Orgreave Close Sheffield S13 9NP
Email: books@bradwellbooks.co.uk
Compiled by Drew Stanton

British Library Cataloguing in Publication Data: a catalogue record for
this book is available from the British Library.

1st Edition

ISBN: 9781909914681

Print: Gomer Press, Llandysul, Ceredigion SA44 4JL
Design by: jenksdesign@yahoo.co.uk/07506 471162
Illustrations: ©Tim O'Brien 2014

Two Winscombe Cricket Club players are chatting in the bar after a match. "So did you have a hard time explaining last week's game to the wife?" says one.

"I certainly did, "says the other," She found out I wasn't there!"

A teacher at a school in Taunton was having a little trouble getting her Year 11 pupils to understand grammar. "These are what we call the pronouns," she said, "We use them with verbs like this: I am, you are, he/she is." The pupils looked at her with glazed expressions.

Trying a different tack, she said, "Lauren, give me a sentence with the pronoun, 'I' in it."

Lauren began, "I is..."

"No, no, no, no, no NO, NO!" shouted the teacher, "Never, 'I is', always, 'I am'... now try again."

Lauren looked puzzled and a little hurt, thought a while then began again more quietly, "I... am...the ninth letter of the alphabet."

Insurance Assessor: "What gear were you in at the moment of the impact?"

Woman Driver: "Gucci sweats and Reeboks."

Two aerials meet on a roof, fall in love, get married. The ceremony was rubbish - but the reception was brilliant.

A young couple decided to go to the Glastonbury Festival for the first time; it was a very in-tents experience

Two rival cricketers from Chew Magna and Wembdon were having a chat.

"The local team wants me to play for them very badly," said the man from Wembdon.

"Well," said his friend, "you're just the man for the job."

A Yeovil housewife went to the greengrocer's. She picked up a lettuce and examined it. "Why is it that these iceberg lettuces just seem to be getting smaller and smaller?" she asked the shop assistant, "Global warming," he replied.

A rather cocky young man, who worked on a busy construction site in Bridgwater, was bragging that he could outdo anyone in a feat of strength. He made a special case of making fun of Morris, one of the more senior workmen. After several minutes, Morris had had enough.

"Why don't you put your money where your mouth is?" he said. "I'll bet a week's wages that I can haul something in a wheelbarrow over to that outbuilding that you won't be able to wheel back again."

"You're on, mate," the over-confident young man replied. "it's a bet! Let's see what you got."

Morris reached out and grabbed the wheelbarrow by the handles. Then, nodding to the young man, he said, "All right. Get in."

A couple from the Frome had been courting for nearly twenty years. One day as they sat on a seat in the park, the woman plucked up the courage to ask, "Don't you think it's time we got married?" Her sweetheart answered, "Yes, but who'd have us?"

A lawyer from Dorchester and a businessman from Taunton ended up sitting next to each other on a long-haul flight.

The lawyer started thinking that he could have some fun at the man from Taunton's expense and asked him if he'd like to play a fun game. The businessman was tired and just wanted to relax. He politely declined the offer and tried to sleep. The lawyer persisted, explaining, "I ask you a question, and if you don't know the answer, you pay me just £5; you ask me one, and if I don't know the answer, I will pay you £500."

This got the businessman a little more interested and he finally agreed to play the game.

The lawyer asked the first question, "What's the distance from the Earth to the moon?"

The man from Taunton said nothing, but reached into his pocket, pulled out a five-pound note and handed it to the lawyer.

Now, it was his turn to ask a question. He asked the lawyer, "What goes up a hill with three legs, and comes down with four?"

The lawyer scratched his head. He looked the question up on his laptop and searched the web. He sent emails to his most well-read friends. He used the air-phone to call his colleagues in Dorchester, but he still came up with nothing. After over an hour of searching, he finally gave up.

He woke up the businessman and handed him £500. The man pocketed the cash smugly and dozed off again.

The lawyer was wild with curiosity and wanted to know the answer. He shook the businessman awake. "Well? What goes up a hill with three legs and comes down with four?" he demanded. The businessman reached into his pocket, handed the lawyer £5 and went straight back to sleep.

Two elderly ladies were enjoying half a cider in their local in Nether Stowey.

One said to the other, "Was it love at first sight when you met your late husband?"

"No, I don't think so," came the reply, "I didn't know how much money he had when I first met him!"

Q: Why did the Somerset farmer's wife go on a diet?
A: She wanted to cheddar a few pounds

A man from Bridgwater said to his wife, "Get your coat on love. I'm off to the club."

His wife said, "That's nice. You haven't taken me out for years."

He said, "You're not coming with me...I'm turning the heating off when I go out."

A bloke from Shepton Mallet goes into an artist's studio and asks if the artist could paint a picture of him surrounded by beautiful, scantily clad women. The artist agrees but he is intrigued by this strange request. He asks his new client why he wants such a picture painted and the bloke says, "Well, if I die before me missus when she finds this painting she'll wonder which one I spent all me money on!"

The next day the bloke's wife goes into the artist's studio and asks him to paint her wearing a big diamond necklace and matching earrings.

"Of course, madam," says the artist, "but may I ask why?"

"Well," replies the woman, "if I die before me husband I want his new woman to be frantic searching for all me jewellery!"

Derek and Duncan were long-time neighbours in Williton. Every time, Derek saw Duncan coming round to his house, his heart sank. This was because he knew that, as always, Duncan would be visiting him in order to borrow something and he was fed up with it.

"I'm not going to let Duncan get away with it this time," he said quietly to his wife, "Watch what I'm about to do."

"Hi there, I wondered if you were thinking about using your hedge trimmer this afternoon?" asked Duncan.

"Oh, I'm very sorry," said Derek, trying to look apologetic, "but I'm actually going to be using it all afternoon."

"In that case," replied Duncan with a big grin, "you won't be using your golf clubs, will you? Mind if I borrow them?"

A lad from Trowbridge who had just started his first term at Sherborne School in Dorset asked a prefect, "Can you tell me where the library's at?"

The older student said disdainfully, "At Sherborne, we never end a sentence with a preposition."

The new boy tried again, "Can you tell me where the library's at, you noggerhead?"

What do you call the two people that always have to embarrass you the most in front of all your friends? Mum and Dad.

A well-known academic from Dorchester was giving a lecture on the philosophy of language at The Bath Literature Festival. He came to a curious aspect of English grammar.

"You will note," said the somewhat stuffy scholar, "that in the English language, two negatives can mean a positive, but it is never the case that two positives can mean a negative."

To which someone at the back responded, "Yeah, yeah."

A Somerset man is driving through Dorset, when he passes a farmer standing in the middle of a huge field. He pulls the car over and watches the farmer standing stock-still, doing absolutely nothing. Intrigued, the man walks over to the farmer and asks him, "Excuse me sir, but what are you doing?"

The farmer replies, "I'm trying to win a Nobel Prize."

"How?" Asks the puzzled Somerset man.

"Well," says the farmer, "I heard they give the prize to people who are outstanding in their field."

A police officer was patrolling the lanes outside Midsomer Norton one night, when he noticed a car swerving all over the road. Quickly, he turned on his lights and siren and pulled the driver over. "Sir, do you know you're all over the road? Please step out of the car."

When the man got out of the car, the policeman told him to walk in a straight line.

"I'd be happy to, offisher," said the drunk, "if you can just get the line to stop moving about."

At a large house in Chard, the doorbell rings. The lady of the house answers the front door to find a man with a toolbox standing on her porch.

"May I help you?" she asks.

"I'm the piano tuner," he says.

"But I didn't send for a piano tuner." she exclaims.

"No," he replies. "your neighbors did."

At a cricket match in Wellington, a fast bowler sent one down and it just clipped the bail. As nobody yelled "Ow's att!" the batsman picked up the bail and replaced it. He looked at the umpire and said, "Windy today isn't it?"

"Yes," said the umpire, "Mind it doesn't blow your cap off when you're walking back to the pavilion."

26

A policeman stops a drunk wandering the streets of Weston-Super-Mare at four in the morning and says, "Can you explain why you are out at this hour, sir?"

The drunk replies, "If I was able to explain myself, I would have been home with the wife ages ago."

What do you get if you cross The Cherries with an OXO cube? A laughing stock.

Sherlock Holmes and Dr. Watson are camping on Exmoor, contemplating a new mystery. After a good meal and a bottle of wine, they lay down for the night, and went to sleep. Some hours later, Holmes awoke and nudged his faithful friend. "Watson, look up at the sky and tell me what you see."

Watson looked up and replied, "I see millions and millions of stars."
"What does that tell you?" asked Holmes.

Watson pondered for a minute. "Astronomically, it tells me that there are millions of galaxies, and potentially billions of planets. Astrologically, I observe that Saturn is in Leo. Horologically, I deduce that the time is approximately a quarter past three. Meteorologically, I suspect that we will have a beautiful day tomorrow. What does it tell you, Sherlock?"

Holmes was silent for a minute, then spoke. "It tells me that someone has stolen our tent."

One freezing cold December day, two blondes went for a walk through Leigh Woods in search of the perfect Christmas tree. Finally, after five hours looking, one turns to the other and says crossly, "That's it, I've had enough. I'm chopping down the next fir tree we see, whether it's decorated or not!"

Miss Malaprop was telling a colleague about the wonderful evening she had had the night before at the ballet at the Theatre Royal Bath. She commented on the wonderful costumes, the fantastic orchestra and, most of all, on how graceful the dancers were, "They just slid across that stage like they were on casternets!"

Did you hear about the magic tractor? It drove up the lane and turned into a field.

An elderly couple from Combe Florey are sitting at the dining table talking about making preparations for writing their wills. Bill says to his missus, Edna, "I've been thinking, my dear, if I go first to meet me maker I don't want you to be on your own for too long. In fact, I think you could do worse than marry Colin in the Chemists or Dave with the fruit stall in the market. They'd provide for you and look after you when I'm gone."

"That's very kind on you to think about me like that, Bill," replied Edna, "But I've already made my own arrangements!"

A reporter from The Clevedon Mercury was covering the local football league match between Watchet Town and Bishops Lydeard. One of the Watchet Town players looked so old he went over to him and said, "You know you might be the oldest man playing in the league. How do you do it at your age?"

The man replied, "I drinks six pints of cider every night, smoke two packets of fags a day, and eat tons of chips."

"Wow, that is incredible!" said the reporter, "How old did you say you were?"

"Twenty-two." said the player proudly.

A Martock couple, Enid and Sidney, are having matrimonial difficulties and seek the advice of a counsellor. The couple are shown into a room where the counsellor asks Enid what problems, in her opinion, she faces in her relationship with Sidney.

"Well," she starts, "he shows me no affection, I don't seem to be important to him anymore. We don't share the same interests and I don't think he loves me at all." Enid has tears in her eyes as the counsellor walks over to her, gives her a big hug and kisses her firmly on the lips.

Sidney looks on in passive disbelief. The counsellor turns to Sidney and says, "This is what Enid needs once a day for the next month. Can you see that she gets it?"

Sidney looks unsettled, "Well I can drop her off everyday other than Wednesdays when I play snooker and Sundays when I go fishing!"

A police officer arrived at the scene of a major pile up on the A37.

The officer runs over to the front car and asks the driver, "Are you seriously hurt?"

The driver turns to the officer and says, "How the heck should I know? Do I look like a lawyer?"

Just before the big race at Wincanton, the trainer was giving last minute instructions to the jockey and appeared to slip something into the horse's mouth just as a steward walked by. "What was that?" inquired the steward.

"Oh nothing," said the trainer, "just a mint."

He offered one to the steward and had one himself. After the suspicious steward had left the scene, the trainer continued with his instructions.

"Just keep on the rail. You're on a dead cert. The only thing that could possibly pass you down the home straight is either the steward or me."

A man went to the doctor one day and said, "I've just been playing rugby for the Vikings and when I got back, I found that when I touched my legs, my arms, my head and everywhere else, it really hurt."

After a careful examination the doctor concluded, "You've broken your finger."

A woman got on a bus in Bridgwater but soon regretted it. The driver sped down the high street, zigzagging across the lanes, breaking nearly every rule of the road. Unable to take it any longer, the woman stepped forward, her voice shaking as she spoke. "You're a shocking driver! I am so afraid of sitting on your bus, I don't know what to do."

"Do what I do," said the bus driver. "close your eyes!"

Did you hear about the idiot who tried to hijack a bus full of Japanese tourists in the Cheddar Gorge? The police had no problem finding him – they had a thousand photographs of the bloke!

A labourer in Taunton, shouted up to his roofer mate on top of an old terraced house, saying, "Don't start climbing down this ladder, Bert."

"Why not?" Bert called back.

"Cos I moved it five minutes ago!" replied his mate.

Sam worked in a telephone marketing company in Trowbridge. One day he walked into his boss's office and said, "I'll be honest with you, I know the economy isn't great, but I have three companies after me, and, with respect, I would like to ask for a pay rise."

After a few minutes of haggling, his manager finally agreed to a 5% pay rise, and Sam happily got up to leave.

"By the way," asked the boss as Sam went to the door, "which three companies are after you?"

"The electric company, the water company, and the phone company." Sam replied.

A bloke walked up to the foreman of a road laying gang in Bridgwater and asked for a job. "I haven't got one for you today," said the foreman, looking up from his newspaper. "But if you walk half a mile down there, you'll find the gang and you can see if you like the work. I can put you on the list for tomorrow." "That's great, mate," said the bloke as he wandered off down the road.

At the end of the shift, the man walked past the foreman and shouted, "Thanks, mate. See you in the morning."
The foreman looked up from his paper and called back, "You've enjoyed yourself then?"

"Yes, I have!" the bloke shouted, "But can I have a shovel or a pick to lean on like the rest of the gang tomorrow?"

A farmer was driving along a country road near the village of Compton Dundon with a large load of fertiliser. A little boy, playing in front of his cottage, saw him and called out, "What do you have on your truck?"

"Fertiliser," the farmer replied.

"What are you going to do with it?" asked the little boy. "Put it on strawberries." answered the farmer.

"You ought to live here." the little boy advised him. "We put sugar and cream on ours."

A young couple were pulling up at their honeymoon hotel in Minehead. The new bride felt very self-conscious about the fact that she was a newly-wed. She turned to her new husband and asked, "What can we do to hide the fact that we are on our honeymoon?"

The young man thought for a second then replied, "I know - you can carry the luggage!"

"I can't believe it," said the American tourist, looking at the grey skies over Weston-Super-Mare, "I've been here an entire week and it's done nothing but rain. When do guys get summer over here?"

"Well, that be hard to say, me old mucker," replied the elderly local. "last year, it were on a Wednesday."

A group hired a Somerset tour guide to drive them around the wildest parts of Exmoor. As night began to fall, they realised that they were really lost.

"I thought you said you knew Exmoor like the back of your hand!" yelled an angry tourist as they drove down yet another dark lane. "I do," replied the tour guide, indignantly, "but I think we're on Dartmoor now."

At The World's End pub in Bradford-on-Tone, a newcomer asked a local man, "Have you lived here all your life?" The old man took a sip of his cider and, after a long pause, replied, "Don't know yet!"

A young couple were doing some shopping in Bath. Having purchased everything they needed, they returned to the car park to drive home.

"Where's the car?" said the wife. "Someone's stolen it!"

They went off to the local police station and reported the theft. Miserably, the couple walked back towards the train station but as they passed the car park, there was their stolen car, back in the exact same spot! On the windshield, there was an envelope. Inside was a note from the thief apologising and saying his wife had gone into labour and he'd just borrowed the car to take her to the hospital. Two tickets to a Wurzels concert were also enclosed as a mark of gratitude.

The young couple's faith in humanity was restored and they went to the concert and had a wonderful time.

They arrive home to Taunton late that night to find that they'd been burgled and the entire contents of their house had been taken. On the front door was a note, which read, "Sorry, but we have to put the kid through university one day."

Did you hear about the last wish of the henpecked husband of a house-proud wife?
He asked to have his ashes scattered on the carpet.

Simon was down on his luck so he thought he would try getting a few odd jobs by calling at the posh houses in Whitestaunton. After a few "no ways", a guy in one of the big houses thought he would give him a break and says, "The porch needs painting so I'll give you £50 to paint it for me."

"You're life-saver, mister," says Simon, "I'll get started right away!" Time passes until…

"There you go, I'm all done with the painting."

"Well, here's your £50," says the homeowner, handing over some crisp tenners.

"Thanks very much," says Simon, pocketing the money, "Oh and by the way, it's a Ferrari, not a Porsche!"

Phil's nephew came to him with a problem. "I have my choice of two women," he said, with a worried frown, "A beautiful, penniless young girl whom I love dearly, and a rich widow who I don't really love."

"Follow your heart," Phil counselled, "marry the girl you love." "Very well, Uncle Phil," said the nephew, "that's sound advice. Thank you."

"You're welcome." replied Phil with a smile, "By the way, where does the widow live?"

At a Somerton school, the maths teacher poses a question to little Josh, "If I give £500 to your dad on 12% interest per annum, what will I get back after two years."

"Nothing," says Josh.

"I am afraid you know nothing about maths, Josh," says the teacher crossly.

"I am afraid too, sir," replies Josh, "you know nothing about my father."

Many years ago there was a dispute between two villages, one in Somerset and the other in Dorset. One day the villagers heard the cry, "One man from Somerset is stronger than one hundred Dorset men."

The villagers in Dorset were furious and immediately sent their hundred strongest men to engage with the enemy. They listened, horrified by the screams and shouts. After hours of fighting, all was quiet but none of the men returned.

Later on, the same voice shouted out, "Is that the best you can do?"

This fired up the people from Dorset and they rallied round, getting a thousand men to do battle. After days of the most frightful blood-curdling sounds, one man emerged from the battlefield, barely able to speak, but with his last breath he managed to murmur, "It's a trap, there's two of them!"

The students from Somerset College were very excited when they got jobs as assistants to the stars, backstage at the Glastonbury Festival. Then they found out that their main task was to help ancient rock stars with their zimmer-frames.

The nervous young batsman playing for Trowbridge Cricket Club was having a very bad day. In a quiet moment in the game, he muttered to the one of his team mates, "Well, I suppose you've seen worse players."

There was no response...so he said it again, "I said 'I guess you've seen worse players'." His team mate looked at him and answered, "I heard you the first time. I was just trying to think..."

A woman from Castle Cary called Carol was still not married at thirty-five and she was getting really tired of going to family weddings especially because her old Aunt Maud always came over and said, "You're next!"

It made Carol so annoyed; she racked her brains to figure out how to get Aunt Maud to stop. Sadly, an old uncle died and there was a big family funeral. Carol spotted Aunt Maud in the crematorium, walked over, pointed at the coffin and said, with a big smile, "You're next!"

For a minute Bournemouth were in with a chance – then the game started.

A tourist drove his flashy Land Cruiser into Cotford St. Luke. He screeched to a halt next to an old local, called Fred.

"Hey you, old man," shouted the tourist, "what's the speed limit in this hick town?"

"We don't have one," said old Fred, "you grockles can't get out of here fast enough for us!"

A pupil at a school in Wells asked his teacher, "Are 'trousers' singular or plural?"

The teacher replied, "They're singular on top and plural on the bottom."

A man rushed into Musgrove Park Hospital and asked a nurse for a cure for hiccups. Grabbing a cup of water, the nurse quickly splashed it into the man's face.

"What did you that for?" screamed the man, wiping his face.

"Well, you don't have the hiccups now, do you?" said the nurse. "No," replied the man. "But my wife out in the car does."

Yeovil Town beat Bournemouth five – nothing; they were lucky to get nothing.

Peter walked up to the sales lady in the clothing department of large shop in Taunton.

"I would like to buy my wife a pretty pair of tights," he said. "Something cute with love-hearts or flower patterns."

"Oh, that's so sweet," exclaimed the sales lady, "I'll bet she'll be really surprised." "I'll say," said Peter, "she's expecting a new diamond ring!"

Did you hear about the fight in the chip shop last week? Six fish got battered!

One day at Yeovil District General Hospital, a group of primary school children were being given a tour. A nurse showed them the x-ray machines and asked them if they had ever had broke a bone.

One little boy raised his hand, "I did!"

"Did it hurt?" the nurse asked.

"No!" he replied.

"Wow, you must be a very brave boy!" said the nurse. "What did you break?"

"My sister's arm!"

A man and his wife walked past a swanky new restaurant in Wells. "Did you smell that food?" the woman asked. "Wonderful!"

Being the kind-hearted, generous man that he was, her husband thought, "What the heck, I'll treat her!"

So they walked past it a second time.

A farmer from Dorset once visited a farmer based near Cheddar. The visitor asked, "How big is your farm?" to which the Somerset farmer replied, "Can you see those trees over there? That's the boundary of my farmland."

"Is that all?" said the Dorset farmer, "it takes me three days to drive to the boundary of my farm."

The farmer from Cheddar looked at him and said, "I had a car like that once."

Did you hear about the truck driver from Trowbridge who was seen desperately chiselling away at the brickwork after his lorry became stuck at the entrance to a tunnel?

"Why don't you let some air out of your tyres?" asked a helpful passer-by.

"No, mate," replied the driver, "It's the roof that won't go under, not the wheels."

Pete and Larry hadn't seen each other in many years. They were having a long chat, telling each other all about their lives. Finally Pete invited Larry to visit him in his new flat in Bridgwater. "I have a wife and three kids and I'd love to have you visit us."

"Great. Where do you live?"

"Here's the address. There's plenty of parking behind the flat. Park and come around to the front door, kick it open with your foot, go to the lift and press the button with your left elbow, then enter! When you reach the sixth floor, go down the hall until you see my name on the door. Then press the doorbell with your right elbow and I'll let you in."

"Great. But tell me...what is all this business of kicking the front door open, then pressing elevator buttons with my right, then my left elbow?"

Pete answered, "Surely you're not coming empty-handed?"

A man from Wambrook bought two horses, but soon realised that he couldn't tell them apart. So he asked the farmer, who lived next door, what he should do. The farmer suggested measuring them. The man came back triumphantly and said, "The white horse is two inches taller than the black horse!"

One day a boy from Dorset was in the back garden shouting, "Mum, why is my Bournemouth top lying on the grass?"His Mum looked out the window and shouted, "The thieving gits stole my pegs!"

A man walks past a pet store in Taunton. There is a sign in the window that says TALKING DOG FOR SALE.

The man doesn't believe it, but he is curious so he goes into the store. He sees a dog, walks up to it and says, "Awright, me old acker?"

The dog says, "Awright, me lover? How be on?"

The man says, "You can really talk!"

The dog says, "That's right, me lover."

The man says, "So what is it like being a talking dog?"

The dog says, "Well, I've lived a gurt life. I rescued Avalanche victims in The Alps. I worked as a drug-sniffing dog for the FBI, and now I read to people in an old folks home five days a week."

The man is absolutely amazed. He turns to the owner of the pet shop and says, "By Jove! Why would you sell a dog like this???" The pet shop owner says, "Because he's a great big liar! He never did ANY of those things."

There were two fish in a tank, one says, "You man the guns, I'll drive."

"You're looking glum", the captain of Bridgwater Cricket Club remarked to one of his players.

"Yes, the doctor says I can't play cricket." said the downcast man.

"Really?" replied the captain, "I didn't know he'd ever seen you play?"

Anne and Matt, a local couple, went to the Trowbridge Village Pump Fair and found a weighing scale that tells your fortune and weight. "Hey, listen to this," said Matt, showing his wife a small white card. "It says I'm bright, energetic, and a great husband." "Yeah," said Anna , "it's got your weight wrong as well."

Supporters, waiting to watch Yeovil Town play Bournemouth, heard that the Cherries were going to be delayed.

They saw a sign on the A37 that said "Clean Lavatories"... so they did.

A Hurrah Henry from Dorset was driving around Trowbridge in his fancy new car and realised that he was lost. The driver stopped a local character, old Tom, and said, "Hey, you there! Old man, what happens if I turn left here?"

"Don't know sir," replied Tom.

"Well, what if I turn right here - where will that take me?" continued the visitor.

"Don't know, sir," replied old Tom.

Becoming exasperated, the driver continued, "Well, what if I go straight on?"

A flicker of knowledge passed over old Tom's face but then he replied, "Don't know, sir."

"I say old man you don't know a lot do you?" retorted the posh bloke.

Old Tom looked at him and said, "I may not know a lot, sir, but I bain't lost like what you are!" With that, old Tom walked off leaving the motorist stranded.

When the manager of Bournemouth started to tell the team about tactics, half the players thought he was talking about a new kind of peppermint.

Down the Nag's Head, a group of blokes sit around drinking when a mobile phone on the table rings. One of the men picks up the mobile and puts the speaker-phone on.

A woman's voice says, "How are you, darling? I hope you don't mind but I've just seen a diamond ring priced £2000 and wondered if I can buy it? I've got your credit card with me."

"Of course, my dear, go ahead," answers the man.

"While I'm on," purrs the lady, "I've noticed a top of the range car I'd like. It's only £65,000, could I order that as well?"

"Of course, my angel," replies the man.

His friends around the table look at each other in disbelief as the lady continues, "And I've just noticed a house with a sea view at Weston-Super-Mare, lover. It's only £750,000 - could we have that as well please?"

"Of course, sugar," answers the man, without so much as blinking.

The phone call is ended and the man smiles at the others and takes a long swill of beer. Then he looks around and shouts "Anyone know whose phone this is?"

A pigeon fancier in Henstridge Village wakes up one morning to find his prize racer has got a wart on its head. Perturbed, he goes to his neighbour to borrow a file.

"What do you want it for?" asks the neighbour. "My pigeon's got a wart on its head. I need to file it off."

"You'll kill it filing its poor little head," says the neighbour. "I won't," replied the fancier, "I know what I'm doing." The next day he goes to return the file and the neighbour asks, "How's the pigeon?"

"He died," replies the fancier sadly. "Told you he would," says the neighbour with some satisfaction. "Oh, it wasn't the filing," replies the fancier, "I think I tightened the vice round his neck too much!"

A golfer was going around the Kingweston Golf Club course. He was talking to his caddy between holes about a forthcoming competition. "I've been drawn against Jack Smith from Dudsbury Golf Club down in Dorset, is he any good?"

The caddy checked for a moment and said, "He's absolutely rubbish. Can't get around the course with any ease. He set a new course record for the worst round ever that has only just been beaten."

"Oh, I should easily get through to the next round then, shan't I?" said the golfer complacently. The caddy looked down at the scorecard and said, "I wouldn't bet on it!"

It was match day for Yeovil Town and excited crowds filled the streets of Yeovil, heading for the stadium. A funeral procession drove slowly through the throng. One of the fans stopped, took off his hat and bowed reverently as the hearse passed. "That was a nice thing to do," remarked his mate.

"Well," said the Yeovil supporter, "she was a good wife to me for thirty odd years."

There's a man in Swanage who claims to have invented a game that's a bit like cricket; what he doesn't realise is Dorset County Cricket Club's been playing it for years.

Darren proudly drove his new convertible into Taunton and parked it on the main street. He was on his way to the recycling centre to get rid of an unwanted gift, a foot spa, which he left on the back seat.

He had walked half way down the street when he realised that he had left the top down with the foot spa still in the back. He ran all the way back to his car, but it was too late...another five foot spas had been dumped in the car.

Ten women out on a hen night in Bridgwater thought it would be sensible if one of them stayed more sober than the other nine and looked after the money to pay for their drinks. After deciding who would hold the money, they all put twenty pounds into the kitty to cover expenses. At closing time after a few white wine spritzers, several vodka and cokes, and a Pina Colada each, they stood around deciding how to divvy up the leftover cash.

"How do we stand?" said Sharon.

"Stand?!" said Debbie. "That's the easy part! I'm wondering how I can walk. I've missed the last bus to North Petherton!"